Best Bitches

Best Bitches

Guide to navigating complicated female relationships!

Meg Glidden, MS, NCC

GLIDDEN BOOKS

WWW.GLIDDENBOOKS.COM

Northwest Florida

First Published September 2013.

ISBN-13: 978-0615887227 (Glidden Books)
ISBN-10: 0615887228

CreateSpace Independent Publishing Platform.
BooksInPrint.com®

Best Bitches: Guide to navigating complicated female relationships Cover and Book Design by Pure Color Web Designs

Please visit us online at www.BestBitchesBook.com

Glidden Books' publications are available through Amazon.com

For further information visit our website at www.GliddenBooks.com

Dedication

To all the beloved bitches
that make my world go 'round:

May we understand ourselves,
And each other better.
Judge each other less,
and maximize the blessing
of being in each other's lives.

Introduction

Ever complicated are the complex minds and emotions of a female. Ask any man that you know, and he will surely be able to validate this as fact. Despite all of their complexities, the bonds between females are socially necessary and vital to the long term happiness of each feminine individual.

Unfortunately, it is common for females to shy away from each other in an attempt to avoid recreating past negative experiences with the ladies in their lives. In order to overcome stereotypical cattiness and continued power struggles to truly engage in the endless potential benefits of these bonds, it is imperative to understand not only what kind of bitch you are, but what kinds of bitches surround you.

We can't change each other but we can gain perspective on how to best use the assets of another female personality to our advantage, without attempting to control her. Once the framework of self-awareness and a willingness to accept others as they are is set, we are able to take these same-sex relationships to a whole new level of fulfillment and satisfaction. Instead of using the term, "bitch" to demean and degrade one another, we start to draw an appreciation for the fire that females radiate as they each try to navigate their lives and thrive in a male dominated world. Whether they are our actual, or simulated, mothers, sisters, daughters, etc., ladies have a special knack for supporting each other in ways that men can't. And of course, after that bonding moment has passed, they are uniquely able to piss each other off beyond belief in the next. Best friends are great, but best bitches are so much better.

Introduction

From the moment that we enter the world, we are special. We are the future creators of the next generation of humanity. We are nurturers. We are caregivers. We are female.

Like it is for all members of the animal kingdom, this designation is not without peril; in order to thrive, we must first ensure our individual survival. We pick up on the nuances of where our culture and environment places us and start to observe very early on how family and friends may treat us differently than our male counterparts. We are exposed to stereotypes and traditions, and as we gain knowledge and increased awareness through age, we start trying to sort out what it all means for us as individual entities.

Despite leaps in feminine equality and society's push to break through outdated gender roles, the undeniable truth is that we are different. We look, develop, and think in ways that diverge from the more linear thoughts of males. While we are certainly capable of doing, being, and achieving the same things that they do, we tend to go about it in a particularly feminine way.

As we create our individual identities, our femininity persists, and can cause problems for us if we are not able to hone it and utilize our differences to our advantage. One area that this becomes most visible in is the way we react to and engage with other females. While men are often stereotyped into the role of innate competitors, there is a reason that the scorned woman is to be feared.

It is my hope that through a greater understanding of the cycles and stages women go through, we can better rally together as a united band of bitches that embrace the complexities of femininity, rather than suffer alone. Let us not avoid the relationships that can best empower us.

The Bitch Cycle

The journey of survival and self-actualization is an ongoing process, full of feminine change. While you may be able to accept that you are a certain breed of bitch now, understand that it is possible to vacillate quickly into another category, based on the situation at hand, or the audience in front of you. In addition, it is also possible to channel several types of bitch at one time.

Keeping this in mind, let's take a look at 17 of the most common brands of bitches that we encounter and/or become; what each bitch stands for, and how to appreciate this bitch for what she is communicating.

Solitary   Ultimate
Sister   Grand
Younger   Micro
Older   Crazy
Insecure   Toxic
Lost   Single
Trench   Married
Co Bitch   Mother
Professional

Judge not the bitch to your right, until you've evaluated the bitch within. Don't shy away from yourself, or the other, because beautiful freedoms and friendships are gained through this understanding.

Solitary Bitch

This bitch shies away from the other females. She's afraid to reach out, for fear of getting burned, and instead retracts within herself. She is prone to surround herself with males because they embrace her without challenge, and do not threaten tapping into old bitch-on-bitch wounds. While she may cultivate her own inner sense of being and develop many skills to help her cope with her lack of feminine connection, she gets lonely. She is likely to have had troubled encounters with females in the past, or had a lack of their presence in her life all together. She avoids other bitches as a means of self-preservation.

If this bitch reaches out to you, pursue her friendship. Don't bombard her with forced interaction, but let her slowly delve into the experience of positive female interaction. Increasing her exposure to healthy females is an integral part of her healing and gaining the strength to overcome the emotional or psychological injuries of past relationships gone awry.

If you are the solitary bitch, know that while it remains true that many   females have the potential to do you wrong, just as many are willing and able to dutifully stand by your side. The only way to earn the benefits of this, are to courageously let your guard down, and try, try again.

Sister Bitch

This bitch is often the initial source of the necessity to develop competitive cattiness with other females. She teaches us how to pounce on the weaknesses of others, and promote ourselves as she challenges our own access to the spotlight.

Her sheer presence in our lives encourages us to pursue our own uniqueness and is a point of contention and comparison right out of the gate. Birth order doesn't matter here because this bitch is on your radar for life, and never goes away no matter how much time or turmoil goes down between you. She can be your nemesis, your cohort, and your hero, all rolled into one.

After we work our way through the childhood developmental stages with her and iron out our conflicts, she often becomes one of the most beloved bitches in our repertoire. She may not understand us best, but this bitch gets the award for being there, for pushing us to continually examine ourselves, and for being someone who has a relationship with you like no other.

Stand with this bitch when she needs you, so that she will be willing to heed your call in your own time of need. The only weapon more lethal to wield against adversaries than the love of a parent, is the camaraderie of a sibling. This bitch is the Calvary- signed, sealed, and delivered out of a lifetime of owning the solitary rights to be your bitch. Have full faith that she will come out with temper blazing when someone else tries to step on her turf.

Younger Bitch

This bitch is a major source of annoying motivation. She reminds us of a life less complicated and a physical presence no longer easily attainable for us. Learn to love her for her honest self-absorption and blissful, inexperienced ignorance. She'll find out soon enough, the lessons that life has in store for her, that the rest of us have already encountered. Never forget that you were once in her shoes, and no matter how you see it, she sees you in the same light that you view your own "older" bitches.

Let this one remind you to still put yourself first sometimes. Let her motivate you to reconnect with mainstream culture and let your hair down once in a while. Be approachable to this one: she needs non-confrontational support and guidance, just like you need a periodic infusion that reconnects you with a zest for things less serious. This relationship is mutually beneficial because she thinks you're weird but interesting, and let's face it; not many people appreciate those nuances as we age.

Don't let jealously or soured judgment cloud your ability to appreciate this bitch. Don't rain on her parade, but instead be there to help her pick up the pieces and push forward when life starts to challenge her delicate psyche.

Older Bitch

This bitch is only difficult when we try to compete with her, or wrestle her for control in the relationship. No competition is necessary; she's you, just in another stage of life. This bitch simply has more time on her side, no matter how you slice it. Learn from her. Chances are, anytime she comes off as condescending, she's reliving her own experiences through you and trying to save your egotistical ass from going down a non-productive path.

It's important to develop respect for this bitch regardless of what you may assume about her. Life is full of curveballs and roadblocks and this bitch has learned through trial and error how to keep surviving no matter what. If she mothers you; take it as a compliment. If she challenges you; try to see it through her eyes, chances are, there's wisdom in the lesson that she's trying to communicate. If she pisses you off; check yourself for potentially juvenile behaviors that she just might be right about. Keep communications honest and free flowing with this bitch – she's often a blessing in disguise.

She will nurture you when you're wounded. She will show up with spirit during major shifts in your life. This is the one that helps you keep   yourself in check. Honor the fact that this bitch has perspective that you won't have for many years, and understand that you can learn and grow from interacting with each other.

Insecure Bitch

As life happens all around us, it becomes apparent that sometimes, who we are today, many not be something that we want to accept, or can even begin to understand. This is a normal process and even the most grounded, headstrong bitch is insecure sometimes.

Nearly all females first experience insecurity during adolescence, and as our identities either falter or bloom, this is not our last encounter with our hypercritical inner critic. This bitch is searching for who she is, or who she wants to be.

She may annoyingly take on some of your traits as her own, or display chameleon like behavior in response to her environment, but temper her. Imitation is a compliment, and it is not likely to last long as she realizes that she may admire certain things about you, but she is unique and can't find solace in styles, hobbies, or personalities that don't accurately reflect her true nature. Be patient with her while she fleshes out who she is and takes root in her own identity.

If you find yourself backsliding into insecurity, take stock in what is the driving force behind it. Take an inventory of what you want, what you're good at, and get started on a solution-focused game-plan to edge your way forward. Identity crisis can be a wonderful opportunity for growth, motivation, and change. Challenge insecurity by evolving into the best you that you can be, in this moment.

Crazy Bitch

This bitch is important. We don't talk to her every day, but we learn to appreciate her special blend of loco for the variety that she brings into our lives. She's the one that we call to let off steam, to cajole someone onto our bandwagon, and to lash out at threatening situations and adversaries when we need a double dose of crazy by our side.

She usually has enough redeeming qualities that you can find likeness and common ground with her, which is the reason that she initially becomes a friend. Her courageous lack of concern with social etiquette and factual logic are intriguing to us and cause us to reexamine the amount of rigidity and conformity that we allow to take hold within ourselves. She becomes an irreplaceable bitch the very first time she backs you up when you stumble and let your own crazy bitch loose (and yes, to be clear, every female has her very own inner crazy that she tries to keep restricted, but has to let out every now and then).

Don't judge this bitch; either she just got tired of beating her inner crazy down, or she really just can't see that she is the way she is. We are all works in progress and this bitch isn't going to put up with shit from you, or anyone else. Temper this bitch. Let her be her, and love her for it. If you don't cultivate a healthy relationship with her and maintain it, she will be sorely missed when you need her.

Lost Bitch

This bitch has likely fallen off the deep end. Sometimes, despite our best efforts, life gets to us, and we react poorly. What may have once been your solid, predictable Bitch, is now doing outrageous, out of character things, and it scares the hell out of you. And you have to let her do them. Let her go there. Let her freak out and release the energy that has become so pent up that she is reacting to her stress this way. You don't have to pretend to agree, or in any way enable the behaviors, but this is her plight, not yours.

Be sure to set boundaries with this bitch, so that you don't get sucked into her chaotic breakdown, but don't turn away. Continue to offer words of encouragement and suggest healthier outlets for stress or sadness (if she solicits them) and pray like hell that she quickly rebounds and finds her way again. Being lost, for any reason, is painful, taxing, and rattles a woman to the core. The only way back to center, is driven from within. When she has arrived at that point, and only then, will your words and efforts not be in vain.

Once she stabilizes, stop looking for the bitch you had in the beginning; she is forever lost to time and trials. Instead, get to know this changed concept of a new bitch evolving right before your eyes. Figure out how your relationship with this bitch needs to grow and change in response.

Trench Bitch

No matter where you are at in life, this bitch is necessary to your ability to function without losing your mind. Whether it's clawing through grad school, establishing your career, or navigating marriage and motherhood, this bitch gets your plight, understands your struggles, and cheerleads you on even though she's also struggling with her own shit.

Females need partners, outside of the romantic variety, and this bitch is your rock. She understands the necessity to trade childcare with you so she can hit the gym twice a week, in exchange for childcare while you take that X-rated, kid free overnight with your hubby once a month.

She has extra individually wrapped snacks when you forget them for your child's field trip and gives you dog food so that you don't have to go back to the store after a horrible day at work. You loan her money if you have it without questions and show up to clean her bathrooms for her when she's having a premenstrual meltdown before her family comes to visit for a week. This bitch isn't competition, she's soul food.

Don't forget to show this bitch your undying appreciation for her presence in your life from time to time: not in exchange for future favors, but because you love and need her. Never lose sight of the revolving balance of kindness and favors between you: she's the buffer between having to rely too much on family or solely your own devices; the buffer between you and the insanity of the expectations that you have levied upon yourself. This bitch is the friendship jackpot - always reciprocate.

Co-Bitch

This bitch is of the educated or experienced, professional variety. These are the ladies that we work with side by side as we stab away at making a living, while also trying to maintain meaningful lives. We keep them close and admire their skills and strengths, and they see us in an appreciative light as we attempt to apply our unique skills and learn from them as we collaborate, create, and succeed together.

These bitches make the day to day life of a working woman tolerable and bring meaning to jobs that may otherwise suck the life out of us if we let them. Whatever diversity of personality and skills these bitches bring into our lives, we cheer each other on by giving one another a safe place for crying and venting behind closed doors. These bitches normalize the roller coaster of stress that you are juggling to make all the facets and ends of your life meet up. Ladies in this bracket are important because they nurture our need to be nurtured and encouraged, in one of the most stressful aspects of our lives. They too are on the journey of challenging themselves to be Debbie-Do-Alls with loud inner critics and perfectionist attitudes. Let the love flow freely to and from them, as they can be the beginning of lifelong connections to friendships that move with you long after one of you has thrown in the towel or been promoted to something bigger or better.

Interaction with the co-bitch is fulfilling and stimulating because they are often fluent in many of your languages- intellectual, crazy, in the trenches, and otherwise. This special breed of a bitch is an undisputed favorite.

Professional Bitch

This is the bitch in charge of you. Love her or hate her, occupational hierarchies demand that someone take the reigns as a leader. Accept your lack of control here. No one gets to start out on top, and whether she's older, younger, insecure, or crazy: she's done something right along the way and that's why you are being demanded to answer to her, instead of the other way around.

Connect instead of competing here. Let this bitch be your guide to achieving whatever it is that you want in the professional arena- whether it's through being an example of what you too are willing to do to reach her status, or not willing to do, she is an invaluable resource of real life application that sparks your own creativity for the formation of your own ideas on how you can or will do it differently. Soak up the exposure that you get to this bitch and take notes.

If you are the top dog, professional bitch, take pride in the fact that your skills and experiences have elevated you to a status that other bitches envy. Stay empowered to lead them. Don't lose sight of what it was like when you were in the trenches like they are now, but aspire to give them what you had to struggle for alone on your journey upwards. You are a successful inspiration to the ranks; push them to maximize their potential and build resiliency in their craft.

Ultimate Bitch

This bitch is another one that we may experience a lot of ebb and flow with. Life changes and pushes you apart for individual growth before pulling you back together based on basic principle. This bitch may, or may not, have much in common with you, but she is the vault. She is the secret keeper, the voice of conscience, and the ultimate consultant. You don't always call her for the day to day, but she's the bitch that understands everything about you, better than you yourself at times. She's the one that's called with major life change: death, divorce, identity crisis, infidelity, career change...whatever it is, if it is that important: this bitch knows about it.

Choose this one carefully, she's not just given to you, she evolves in your life before she is selected for long term friendship marriage. This   relationship needs to be for life. Make sure that you and this bitch have a mutual understanding. Be prepared to give just as much to her, as you take from her. In the female hierarchy, she's easiest maintained outside of your regular estrogen-filled circle because even though it can be fun to integrate her from time to time, your other bitches will always see her as competition, and she will always win. This bitch is the fine china, and the buck stops with her. She's the final say, the indispensable, irreplaceable, bottom-bitch that's always on top.

Grand Bitch

This bitch is the wisest of us all. Time has either softened her or made her sassier than ever. She gets to say whatever she wants, judge us each, and smile fondly about our plights and frustrations. She's seen it all, done it all, and lived long enough to watch us blunder along in a long line of learning experiences. She has overcome the need for competition and has phased out of needing us, the way that we need each other. She's been every kind of bitch there is, she's loved and lost her bitches along the way, and now she's on cruise control.

There is so much to learn from this one, but seldom will we realize it until she's gone and we achieve her status. We may pawn her off as being outdated, but she knows that even though times may change, it doesn't matter if you're a woman in the 1920s or the 2020s, context doesn't change our innate feminine psyche: Social norms don't change our hormonal urges, and cattiness, whether in a written letter, email, or text message; it all translates the same. She's relinquished the struggles for acceptance and achievement and has now gained the all-knowing perspective of seeing everything in hindsight. Infinite gratitude and respect to this bitch.

Micro Bitch

This bitch is the scariest of them all. These are the ones that test us, try us, and challenge us beyond all reproach. When she's young, we want her to submit to us, perhaps our most futile conquest, yet she never really will. We want to groom her to perfection, save her from hurts, mistakes, and disappointments, yet we cannot. We love her more than any other bitch, and many times she will be adamant that we hate her. When we look at her, we are forced to accept that it's like gazing into a time-lapsed mirror of what our adult bitch may have acted like as a child. She is of our own making.

Despite our approach or intentions, she will grow, and change, and develop into her own special kind of bitch that we never lose hope or faith in. She will judge us more harshly than any other, she will cut us to the quick, and we will take it, because this bitch owns us, no matter how hard we try not to let her. If we are lucky, she may truly appreciate us one day, but only when she's ready, and that will come on her own terms, when even she least expects it.

The micro bitch is to be adored. She is undiluted with reality and prospers within our shadow until it is time for her to surpass it. She is the unique embodiment of the precious line of bitches next in line for the throne.

Toxic Bitch

Acceptance of self and others, the way they are, not the way you want them to be, is the key to success in a life full of bitches. But the toxic bitch is where we have to draw the line.

This bitch is conniving, manipulative, opportunistic, and will wreak havoc if you let her. She ropes you into drama, disregards your boundaries, and tries to infiltrate your thoughts to her advantage. There is no reciprocity here. Whether she came by it honestly through negative experiences or role models, or has been turned by abuse or addiction: you can't save, change, or temper her. Give her resources to know how to access help if you can, and then let her walk away with her anger, jealousy, promiscuity and/or other problems. After all, she's the only one that can set her course onto a different path.

If this bitch is someone you care about, get comfortable with the concept of tough love and set hard limits that protect your own sense of safety. Although this can feel heartbreaking in the moment, remember that if she knows you will tolerate it, what on earth is her incentive to change? Allow yourself to retain love for the toxic bitch, but only from a distance.

If you are a toxic bitch, don't despair. Identifying what your issues are and where they came from, is the first step in breaking away from the bondage of a toxic lifestyle. It can and will get better if you are dedicated to learning new skills and applying them for positive change. Changes may not be visible right away, but the second you commit to overcoming dysfunction, your spirit is filled with a new sense of hope. Seek positive people, support groups, and therapy if you need it; a happier, healthier you is just over the horizon.

Single Bitch

Obviously, we aren't born with a leading romance in our lives. Sometimes, finding that special someone isn't that easy, and God forbid you find one but your "Love" turns out to be a loser. It's complicated enough to figure out how we relate to each other, but it's important take into consideration how our mindset over, and potential pursuit, of love can change platonic female-on- female dynamics. The single bitch may, or may not, be looking for romantic companionship and that is totally her prerogative. We have to figure out where her place is within our circle.

Singles bitches can be a blessing, or a curse, depending on where you are with your own relationship status. If you too are single: she's a godsend who shares the same kind of freedom to drop everything at a moment's notice for an impromptu adventure. If you are relationally attached, your allegiance to her must come second, or risk causing disruption to your primary commitment. Wherever she falls on your spectrum, be patient and attentive. There's always room for her, but boundaries and mutual understandings are key.

If you are a single bitch: enjoy the freedom. Romantic love falls into place over time and it is well worth waiting for the right opportunity to come along before you seize it. Remember, while you definitely don't need a romantic partner to survive, this person can love and fulfill you in ways that your staple bitches can't. Make sure that you are whole long before romance starts to dominate the equation.

Married Bitch

This bitch has identified a companion. She's committed to navigating the long term push and pull of a romantic relationship. Love or hate her Chosen, they are now part of the package that you must temper in order to keep your relationship with this bitch alive. Creating conflict with her companion causes more struggle than it's worth. Even if you can't find it within yourself to respect the companion, respect the judgment, desires, and decisions of your bitch.

Total integration is not necessary here and rarely even recommended. In response to the merger of marriage, it is your job to assist your bitch in staying grounded in her own identity as an individual, outside of the communal relationship. You remain a confidant, a treasure, an outlet, and an important piece of the puzzle, even if it isn't in the spotlight here. Don't be threatened by the love of her life, and be careful not to judge (or at least don't do it out loud).

If you are a married bitch, don't lose sight of the importance of maintaining your bitch circle. Long term, romantic love can be wonderful, but should not become the all-consuming focus of your identity. Instead, value your marriage for the blessings that it brings into your life, but stay in touch with who you are, both outside of the marriage, and inside of the bitch collective.

Mother Bitch

This bitch is a force to be reckoned with. She has tapped into a vitally primal source of her femininity and you can bet your ass she will never stop fighting tooth and nail for her cause. Embarking on motherhood has an instinctual and profound effect on bitches. This is perhaps, as real as it gets. Pushing her body, mind, and emotions to the max from the moment of conception and throughout the rest of her lifetime, this bitch has conviction.

She's still that graduated micro bitch evolving into her own, but the deeply rooted genetic code of her femininity has now conjured the inner nurturer, protector, and fighter to the surface. This bitch can be gentle and inviting but watch yourself- this bitch has a mission, a purpose, and she will lash out viciously if you start to impose judgment or threat; to her or her offspring. Here, we learn to let the mother bitch do exactly what it is that she does, and we let her do it her way while we chose wisely to steer clear of a stand-off.

When you are this bitch, you gain perspective: once you unlock the mother bitch within, there is no going back. Embrace her, admire her, and wield her instincts wisely. Understand that those who have not experienced this process cannot fully understand it, and even your peers who have are likely to view it differently; and that's okay.

Who's my Bitch

As we walk through the ages and stages of the bitch cycle, things start to fall into place. We can see where our personal path has led us all across the spectrum, and no matter where you fall on any given day, those inner brands of bitch are still walking with you.

Allow this process to increase your insight, wisdom, and improve your ability to connect with other bitches. If you believe in the saying, "it takes a village to raise a child," recognize that you will forever be that child, and you will always need the village to raise you up when you are down.

Judge not the bitch to your right,

Until you've evaluated the bitch within.

Don't shy away from yourself,

or the other,

Because beautiful freedoms and friendships

Are gained through this understanding.

Communication 101

- Communication, by nature, indicates that there is both a source, and a recipient of information, on a two way street.

- If you don't say exactly what you mean, feel, or think: everyone else is just guessing.

- Listening requires only the attention of your ears, not the movement of your mouth. Learn to wait your turn.

- When you are caught up in the emotions of the moment, you are not capable of thinking logically at that time.

- The quality of communication between you and your bitches is much more important than the quantity.

- Standing by your bitch is an action that communicates support and solidarity. Standing up for her too soon is an insult to her capabilities.

You Need to Recognize

Men will never fully understand what goes on between you and
your bitches - And they don't have to.

When a bitch asks you for advice;
She's not going to take it.
She's going to take it into consideration,
and will end up doing what she damn well pleases.

Saying, "I told ya so,"
turns your bitches away from you.
Opt for, "Damn, B. that's too bad.
What do you want to do now?" instead.

Learn and grow from your arguments;
you're not gonna change that bitch,
and she's not going to change you.

Life without bitches is lonely:
trust that.

All bitches are at least a little crazy,
even you.

Nobody in this world has got your back
the way your bitches do.

Enjoy your inner and outer bitches –

They are the jewels of feminine complexity.

Good Luck Bitch!

www.ingramcontent.com/pod-product-compliance
Lightning Source LLC
Chambersburg PA
CBHW060559030426
42337CB00019B/3576